I0191417

What Still Lingers

Nia Khire

BookLeaf Publishing

India | USA | UK

Made with ❤ on the BookLeaf Publishing Platform
www.bookleafpub.in
www.bookleafpub.com

Dedication

Dedicated to everyone and everything who I turned into my muse

Preface

A collection of all that lingers... -in the labyrinth of the mind, in the creases of the soul.
Poetry that doesn't necessarily focus on closure, but rather on the liberating feeling of having expressed.

Acknowledgements

I started writing poetry around 4 years ago, and I am
completely aware that I have barely scratched its surface.
My first poem stemmed from an attempt to complete an
assignment that I procrastinated on for a month. After I
finished writing it, I realised that words carry immense
power. They hold the truth. They stay with you.
Then I went on several writing journeys...I wrote about
nature and death, then moved on to more metaphorical,
free-verse poetry.
I extend my gratitude to all those who give my poetry
meaning, be it the people I talk to, or the nature that
surrounds me...all of my muses have shaped me.
The very notion of poetry deserves much more credit than
humanity gives it, for with it comes a realisation of
freedom.
Lastly, I'd like to thank the readers. I hope you find a part
of yourself in these poems.

1. Love Chases Me

Love knocks at my door,
Inside my abode chaos ensues.
My feet rooted to the ground of despair-
My hands, bound to shackles of fear,
My lips, sealed shut, the key of fate thrown away-

She calls out to me once more,
I can't respond back, even if I want to.
I know not much about her-
Yet I know enough to be afraid.
She breaks down my walls, she frees me-

Reluctantly I let her hold my hand.
She tends to my wounds, but the pain heightens.
She sings me to sleep, but what follows is unending
nightmares.
I shiver with the coldness my hopelessness brings,
She embraces me.

I push her away and in an instant-
Remorse strikes my soul.
I beg her to stop caring for me-
I beg her to give me peace,
I beg her for forgiveness.

I seek love's advice yet I'm afraid to talk to her-
I fear the mirror that she shall show.
Love understands me and her intentions I fail to
decipher.
With a fond smile she leaves me be-
I scream, for her to help,
-at myself for letting her go again.
I yearn for love but loathe her presence,
I try to heal yet my medicine tastes like poison.

2 . Mother

Mother...feel my sorrow.
I don't want to hurt you,
all I want to do is to make you aware,
of what you have caused.

It is not about what you did.
Perhaps I am what I am,
because of the voice within me.
Mother...protect me.

I drive myself insane-
Trying to free you,
from this prison you created.
Mother...help me.

I fret over you every now and then,
all just to find myself...
stuck in a pointless loop.
Mother...love me.

I feel anxious-
I feel as though- you regret nurturing me.

I never feel enough for you.
Mother...heal me.

3. The End Was Where We Began

The end was where we began-
blissfully unaware, perhaps blatantly ignorant
of the fact that destiny held in its merciless hands,
shards of hopelessness and longing.
Trust me, I could walk on these shards for a million
miles-
all, just to get to you.
Yet, this solitary thought plagues my mind-
"Will you accept me with feet all bloody?
With my skin marred with wounds?
With sheer emptiness in my eyes?"
Then again,
Why would you do all of that for me?
After all, I was discarded.
And for this emptiness I feel,
you created it.

4. Bella

I know not why you left
I know not why I cared so much
Bella, I found solace in your existence.
Come back.

Bella, those innocent eyes,
they used to radiate love
Did you have the same playful smile–
when death reached out his hands to you?

Did you welcome him with open arms
-as though you sensed that he needs love too?
Bella, were you too naïve?
Or were you simply too pure to even exist?

Are you a figment of my imagination-
A creation to console loneliness?
Did even the notion of you decide to leave me–
with gut wrenching grief...and guilt.

Why was I not there for you?
Bella, forgive me.
I could never give you
everything you deserved.

5. Unfinished poetry feels like twilight

Unfinished poetry feels like twilight.

The uncertainty–

of the dusk that lingers amidst the sunset's hues,

of abandoned words that were once filled with potential.

And perhaps the uncertainty was meant to be–

Like that of flickering candlelight,

Or that of the soft rain that fondly teases the window.

The uncertainty is mesmerising.

–and momentary.

The beauty of twilight disappears as the night unveils its dreamy facade.

The allure of half-finished poems is shattered upon the realisation–

of the poet's purpose lost with the search for the perfect metaphor.

6. Ashes Of Peace

I want to burn this house to the very ground.
-and weep, burying myself in its ashes.
I do not want a single soul to hear my wails,
Yet I crave a tender embrace.
I want to heal,
Yet I find comfort in picking at my wounds.
For the presence of pain makes me believe,
That I possess the ability to feel love, should it ever come
my way.
I want to bask in the light the embers would provide,
Yet I find solace in the hesitant moonlight.
I seek the warmth of the flames,
Yet I yearn for winter's cold caress.
And perhaps I shall rue ever laying my eyes on fire,
-and drown in a peaceful slumber having succumbed to
the voice within.

7. I Can't Breathe

I can't breathe.
My past smothers me.
-and the uncertainty of my future,
It makes me want to drown.
I stare at my hands,
they're turning pale,
...I can't feel them,

I surrender myself,
to the wall I lean against.
I never noticed... how much I liked this feeling,
-how much comfort I found in its coldness.

I pry my eyes open.
A futile attempt as I cling onto the last strand of hope.
I can't leave, not right now.

I anticipate "life" to flash before me.
I prepare to bask in memories I get to relive one last
time.
Yet all I am reminded of,
are my mistakes.
Wasn't this supposed to feel liberating?

8. The Obsession with Perfection

Midas' greed,
Patroclus' love,
Heracles' might,
Stand defeated before my desire to suffice.

...and perhaps my obsession with perfection takes a toll
on me,
Perhaps it is concerning,
Or plainly stupid.
Yet I yell to the world till my lungs are devoid of air.
I yell, "My obsession was never innate"
It was fed to me gradually.
My obsession is the dose of poison slipped into every
triumph of mine.

9. Monsoon Skies

Monsoon skies shake me to the very core.
Their intentions? Unpredictable.
To nurture?
To entertain?
To threaten?
The lightning is a daunting code to decipher.

A part of me finds comfort in its mere presence.
Yet a part of me becomes restless by its very thought.
Why do I fear lightning?
Am I not ready for its glory?

Perhaps lightning exists to show me,
The monsoon has my back.
The skies look over me.
The skies care.

10. How To Kill A Poet

Suffocate them by telling them they're worthy.
Collect their tears on your sleeve and kiss it tenderly.
Gaze at them fondly whilst they ponder upon the
universe.
Tell them you love them and then-
Leave.

Ensure that you leave behind,
The taste of the coffee you loved,
The last few lines of the song you always hummed,
The scent of the perfume you never went out without...
-it still stings them...
Slowly, painfully.
The guilt becomes unbearable to them.
They might reach out a hopeful hand.
Caress it for a moment,
Gently...push it away.
That's it.

You've become poetry.
You're immortal.
Two birds in one stone.
You might argue,
"Didn't I make them a better poet?"

That's where the twist comes into play.

Do they seem to have healed?
Has time done its magic?
Turn it into a curse.
Bump into them on a seemingly random Friday evening–
Perhaps at the coffee shop you used to meet at,
Yes, the one where you gave them the two sunflowers.
The one where they told you their deepest fear–
Losing you.
The one they just found the courage to visit again.

Smile as though nothing ever happened,
Do you find joy–
watching the color rise to their cheeks?
Hearing them stutter with disbelief?
Noticing how their eyes still light up the same,
This time with a touch of hope?

Catch up maybe.
Try and show interest, if you're merciful.
Order a different drink,
Say how you can't stand your old favourite now.
Make them question whether they really ever knew you.

You've dug the dagger deep enough now,
Twist it.

With tales of how you've changed,
And how you hated your past,
And how you want to leave it all behind.
Tell them, they don't seem to have changed a bit.

If they ever notice your motive,
And confront you...
How do you respond?
With hatred? Disgust? Rage?
How elementary...

To deliver the final blow
Respond with indifference.
You've numbed their soul,
You've killed the emotions within them.
They have lost their flare.

You shattered the last bits of their sanity.
They're gone.
Yet, after all of that,
Their soul will find you...
Embrace you, and–
Thank you.

11. Judith

She's delicate
She's eternal...
She isn't afraid of bloodshed.
Her blade gleams with purpose.
She is unfazed.
She strikes.

Oh Judith,
I see a hint of confusion in those sharp eyes.
As if you're pondering upon how all of this matters,
As if you wonder whether your worth is defined by the
sword you wield.
Do they really matter-
The bloodstains on your dress?
The whispers of death,
that lurk around in that fleeting moment?
You press on,
Unflinching.

The trophy you bear isn't much of a burden,
But the questions that came along with it-
They seem to crumble your triumphant mind.
Judith, what you did was no easy feat,
You must rest.

You deserve peace.

12. The Swan

He yearns to hear the shotguns echo faintly near the
lake,
Just as they once did when he had finally found
contentment.
As of now, the ripples have lost their playfulness,
The rustling of leaves which once brought a sense of life,
today possess an unsettling eeriness.

The other creatures have found a new sanctuary,
No one dares venture into the tranquil waters–
ever since the lake turned crimson.
Yet his solace lies in the abandoned depths,
–It lies within the love he once called his.

His wails have gone in vain,
For his lover's lifeless eyes gaze right past his soul.
He consoles himself and says, "At least those eyes have
found the tranquility they always longed for."

Every waking day he waits helplessly for time to work
its charm–
And he carries...on his ivory wings, the final gift of his
love.
Blood, that carried promises of eternity–

And tears–
At the tragedy of how fragile it truly is.

13. Braiding The Labyrinth

Rapunzel Rapunzel, let down your hair,
Let down the walls of this tower–
that you built with your very own hands,

Rapunzel Rapunzel, what have you become?
You flinch at the mention of a mother's warm embrace,
"My tresses keep me warm enough"
You tell me whilst caressing those locks–
that you believe, define your worth.

Rapunzel Rapunzel, how do I find the heart to tell you–
This hair,
that you find so precious,
–that brings you ecstasy
As you watch it grow ceaselessly,
Is weaving a labyrinth around you.
Perhaps you have known this
And you find it amusing.
Perhaps you find pleasure in testing,
where the line blurs,
Between exercising freedom,
And losing awareness

Rapunzel Rapunzel, let me braid your hair-

Let's pick out flowers to ornament it,

while we talk,

about whether you really feel like you have it in control,

Or if you think all of this would have been different

had you cared for yourself more,

And maybe later,

you can tell me

if you're finally ready

to let go.

14. Cradled By The Frost

My muse has arisen from her slumber.
Her cold whispers breathe life into my art.
She hums softly to the bluebird's song,
-her arms gently cradling my somnolent soul.

Adorned with hints of indicolite,
She floats like a daydream.
She dances with the bracing breeze,
I wonder what melodies bring out such grace-

She writes through me,
poems of frost-kissed dreams left abandoned.
She revives parts of me that Summer killed,
Her cool caress mending every ache left behind.

15. The Clouds Are Falling

The clouds are falling.

Almost as if to engulf the Earth in a cold embrace.

They're getting closer-

I see them reach out their misty hands,

They caress the Earth gently,

and strangle it.

Is this how it all ends?

Why is it so beautiful?

Why do I not want it to be swift and painless?

Why does the soul yearn to savor every moment of loss?

16. Flames

Flames captivate me,
they possess an aura-
one that could tenderly cleanse,
and in a fit of rage, reduce to ashes.

They know of my envy...
and flaunt their freedom spiritedly.
So formless yet so dignified,
so wild yet so aware-
They are all I yearn to be.

I can't help but wonder why,
they push me away when I approach them.
Flames hurt me.
Flames heal me.
Flames awaken the arsonist within

17. Puzzle Pieces

I would give up on jigsaw puzzles half-way,
Perhaps because I knew what it would turn out like.
The pieces—
their irregularities often amused me,
-perhaps even those irregularities were destined to be
harmonic.

Maybe, my yearning for the unknown got the best of me,
Maybe predestined endings never set me pondering.

How I wish to complete my old puzzles again,
-to start afresh, create a world from memories left
untouched
and—
Find in the final picture,
The missing pieces of myself.

18. Speaking With Your Eyes

Eyes...they're complex.
They spill secrets that words attempt to hide
They offer a peephole into the soul.

Attaining mastery in the art of eye contact is truly a
blessing.
It gives us a sense of individuality and a sense of
belonging, simultaneously.

Our existence is generally deemed insignificant,
Often...by measuring it against that of celestial giants.
Every now and then, we are told of how trivial it truly is
But, the beauty and meaning that it holds,
dawns upon us when we find the eyes of ones we love,
gravitating towards us in a room full of people.

Eyes are our rawest outlet,
be it for ecstasy, grief...and everything in between.

But perhaps,
the reliability of deciphering the language of the eyes...
depends on our willingness to unlearn "societally
accepted" cues

-and look at people as individuals
each operating in their own way.

19. An Unfortunate Metamorphosis

Often, I find myself spiraling into the past,
Grasping at any loose threads of memories
-and trying to weave a reality of my own.

While I gaze upon these strands in my palms,
They slip away,
And drift around me
Taking the shape of words I wish I said

Those words- they echo through me,
Filling spaces that I wish were silent.

Until, all I am reduced to,
is the sum of the words I left unsaid.

20. The Touch Of Dawn

I want the dawn to love me-
The way old souls love the moon.
The way the ocean loves the seabed.
Eternally, unconditionally, completely.

The gentle breeze caresses me till I feel safe.
The skies softly smile at my dazed eyes.
The dawn accepts me-
It accepts me despite reckless mindnights.

Do love and acceptance have a fine line in between?
For I feel as though,
-as though I have been tracing its path,
ever since I first witnessed the dawn.

21. Hiraeth

I want to go back to when my biggest fear was spiders
and not mediocrity.
-back, to when home was a triangle on top of a square by
a dark blue waterfall on a paper.
What I would give,
To write about nature again and not about tears or words
I leave unsaid.
I want to go back to when I could surrender myself to a
song played in public without giving a care of who is
watching,
-to when a road riddled with potholes brought a thrill
and not a surge of agitation.
-to when there was a straightforward answer to "What is
home?"
There are so many answers to that question,
But all of them boil down to one concept-
Home is where you feel enough,
A place to perhaps be conscious of the present-
May that be in the comfort of your room, reading a good
book or humming along to your favorite song...
Or perhaps in the moment where an animal or person
finds solace in your company.
Home can be found in absolute solitude or when
surrounded by those you love.

It is a notion that is ever-changing,
Maybe that's why we tend to feel a bit homesick every
once in a while.
The longing for peace lingers quietly in the back of our
minds all the time,
And perhaps it reflects in the little things that we do.
I want to go back to when art and expression were
considered as human qualities and not skills that only a
few can acquire.
-to when parks gave me happiness because visiting them
was a part of my routine and not because of the
nostalgia that hits me upon using the swing sets (it still
feels just as liberating)
I want to go back to where everything I was would
suffice for me to live with myself.
I want to be one with the stardust that created us.

www.ingramcontent.com/pod-product-compliance
Lightning Source LLC
Chambersburg PA
CBHW050959030426
42339CB00007B/400